HEIRLOOM

HOUSES

HEIRLOOM

THE ARCHITECTURE OF WADE WEISSMANN

HOUSES

WRITTEN BY
STEVEN STOLMAN

GIBBS SMITH
TO ENRICH AND INSPIRE HUMANKIND

CONTENTS

PREFACE, BY WADE WEISSMANN	6
THE ARCHITECTURE OF WADE WEISSMANN	8
ACKNOWLEDGMENTS	11
CREDITS	13
SHINGLE STYLE ON GENEVA LAKE	15
CABIN RETREATS	37
LODGE BY THE LAKE	51
MIDWEST LAKE HOUSE	71
GARDEN FOLLY AND ESTATE RENOVATION	87
NEW-FASHIONED FARMHOUSE	101
SPRAWLING SHINGLE	117
SHINGLE SUMMERHOUSE	135
CONTEMPORARY FOLK	151
COTTAGE ROMANTIC	169
ENGLISH COUNTRY COASTAL	181
HOUSE FOR ALL SEASONS	193
NORTH SHORE CLASSIC	205
FRENCH COUNTRY HOUSE	219
HOUSE ON THE PRAIRIE	227
BEYOND HOUSES	235
URBAN GLAMOUR	235
ERIN HILLS GOLF COURSE	249
GERMAN EQUESTRIAN ESTATE	261

PREFACE

BY WADE WEISSMANN

One of the greatest gifts I was given as a child was the opportunity

to spend time with my family at our hobby farm in Door County, Wisconsin. The 1860s farmhouse and neighboring outbuildings had been constructed utilizing local materials and traditional building methods; and having been laid gently in harmony with the surrounding landscape, each building was marked by a richness and depth that bewildered my senses and fascinated me no end. To this day, I often reflect on the days and nights I spent on that farm and what made them so special to me. I think about how those crude, rustic structures felt in different light, seasons, and function, and how the natural elements and materials blended so seamlessly together to create a uniquely warm, welcoming environment for my family and me.

Just as a film director positions a scene within a specific space in order to heighten the dramatic effect, architectural design, for me, is an opportunity to fashion a space in a manner that will set the stage for the theater — the living — that will one day take place there. As I approach a project, I begin by examining the contextual layers that encompass and envelop the already existing site. I explore the slope of the land, the foliage, the soil, the exposure to wind, the available light, and any neighboring scenery or structures. Even the remnants of previous structures and construction methods, sprinkled like seeds of inspiration on and throughout a site, serve as insight for the design journey.

Alongside those natural, tangible elements lies the history of the site, just waiting to be uncovered, to be intimately known. Who inhabited this space in previous decades? In preceding centuries? What role did this particular space play within a larger cultural and historical context? What were its uses?

And finally, there are the individual stories and personalities of the people who will soon come to occupy this space. What is it that inspired them to want to begin walking out their unique life journeys in this particular space? How do they picture themselves gathering with loved ones for holidays and milestone celebrations? What sensation or emotion do they want to experience as they move from room to room? What are their morning rituals? Their daily routines? And how do they enjoy settling in at the end of an event-filled day?

For me, good architecture is the sum of all of these parts, for it is in the answers to these questions that I find the inspiration to begin exploring not only aesthetic opportunities but also the manner in which those opportunities will be brought to fruition. Creating a plan that will take full advantage of the topography, surrounding views, and natural light; selecting appropriate building materials, along with the type of perspective and artistry that will best put forth the overall design vision — all of these decisions, for me and my team, make up the often complex yet deeply rewarding process of architectural design.

At the end of the day, an architect is nothing if not a storyteller. In the thoughtful creation of a beautiful space, we are inviting history to begin etching itself slowly onto the floors, ceilings, and walls of the built environment.

I wake up every morning and consider it a privilege and blessing to have been gifted with the opportunity to play a role in such a uniquely beautiful, life-affirming process.

Here's to the stories yet to be told and the memories yet to be made.

— Wade Weissmann

THE ARCHITECTURE
OF WADE WEISSMANN

The houses we choose to live in say a great deal about our lives.

For those who are fortunate to work with an architect to design and build a house from scratch, it is one of life's rarest indulgences.

Architects who specialize in bespoke houses are a unique breed and generally subscribe to two wildly opposite philosophies. There are the single-minded architects who demand that the clients mold themselves to fit the architect's specific vision. Indeed, clients look to those architect for direction and, in many cases, definition. Then there are the intuitive architects — ones who absorb the nuances of the client and respond with solutions based on looking and listening. Wade Weissmann is such an architect. He is neither a modernist nor a traditionalist, but rather a lyricist. His houses flow with rhythmic ease, embracing the terrain while gently welcoming the inhabitants. In a world of too many houses built from the inside out, Wade Weissmann's houses exemplify the harmonic resolution between interior and exterior, form and function. They aren't built at once; they are built at last.

This philosophy defines the concept of the heirloom home — houses to live and grow in, to laugh in and cry in, to provide that all-important shelter from the storms of life while reflecting the personalities of those living within them. From his sophisticated manor houses to his modest lakeside cabins, Wade's appreciation for excellence and permanence is apparent. These are houses built to last for generations, to be loved a whole life long.

ABOUT THE ARCHITECT

Wade Weissmann believes that houses should be living scrapbooks capable of telling epic tales about individuals and families. Growing up in the leafy suburbs just north of Milwaukee, Wisconsin, he knows a thing or two about the importance of family and friends, of whom he is blessed aplenty. The son of a commercial artist and a photographer, he graduated from Homestead High School and went on to earn his bachelor of science in architecture from the University of Wisconsin and his master of architecture from the University of Pennsylvania. He is a member of the American Institute of Architects, the National Council of Architectural Registration Boards, and the Institute of Classical Architecture & Art.

"I grew up in a cookie-cutter midcentury ranch," he reveals. But it was his family's "farm" on a peninsula jutting out into the majesty of Lake Michigan, about a three-hour's drive from Milwaukee, that inspired his love and curiosity for structures with age and patina. "I loved the old farm buildings and the grand old houses on Cottage Row in Fish Creek," he says. Founder's Square, a jumble of nineteenth-century residential cottages that now house quaint shops, enthralled him. "The details — the soul of these humble structures — they told such rich stories."

Indeed, it is the storytelling aspect of architecture that defines Wade Weissmann's career and the houses that he and his eponymous firm design with impressive passion and skill. Like beautiful music, a Wade Weissmann house is composed of notes and expressions, rhythm and syncopation, moving forward in time and space towards a resolution that separates ordinary architecture from extraordinary architecture: harmony.

ACKNOWLEDGMENTS

No life or body of work exists in a vacuum, and the projects illustrated in this book are the combined efforts of many lives, artists, craftspeople and collaborators. To thank everyone individually would be impossible, but I would like to generally acknowledge the many lives that helped bring this piece of work to life.

To our clients, I cannot thank you enough for the faith that you placed in our vision and for your willingness to embrace the individuals needed to carry out the very best in construction.

To my WWA family of architects and designers, thank you for lending your skills, talents, collaborations and time to our efforts. You all mean the world to me.

To the team that helped create this book, including Gibbs Smith Publisher, writer Steven Stolman, and my internal creative team, thank you for bringing this dream of mine to fruition.

To my dear cousin, the late designer Jon Schlagenhaft, your presence in my life continues to influence my passion and my work, and so it is to you that I lovingly dedicate this book.

The extraordinary efforts that made this endeavor possible required unending, dedicated love and understanding from my family — brother Brian, sister Jennifer, father Wolfgang, and late mother "Babs" — and friends, all of whom supported and promoted me through the highs and lows, full of faith that my love for, and dedication to, the practice of architecture would one day yield something worthwhile. To all of you, from the bottom of my heart, thank you.

Finally, to my partner and best friend, Matthew Moran, for your unending patience, wisdom, faith and love, thank you.

— Wade Weissmann

CREDITS

Shingle Style On Geneva Lake, pages 14–35
    CONTRACTOR Engerman Contracting
    LANDSCAPE ARCHITECT Scott Byron & Co.
    INTERIOR DESIGN Tina Simmonds of Simmonds
        Design; Robert Alt of Studio Beppa, Ltd.
    PHOTOGRAPHERS David Bader and Matt Moran

Cabin Retreats, pages 36–49
    CONTRACTOR Ruvin Brothers
    LANDSCAPE ARCHITECT Wade Weissmann
    INTERIOR DESIGN Wade Weissmann/
        Jon Schlagenhaft
    PHOTOGRAPHER David Bader

Lodge by the Lake, pages 50–69
    CONTRACTOR Engerman Contracting
    LANDSCAPE ARCHITECT Scott Byron & Co.
    INTERIOR DESIGN Emily Winters and Jennifer Schupie
        of Peabody's Interiors
    PHOTOGRAPHER David Bader

Midwest Lake House, pages 70–85
    CONTRACTOR Barenz Builders
    LANDSCAPE ARCHITECT Landworks, Inc.
    INTERIOR DESIGN Beth Wangman of I4Design
    PHOTOGRAPHER David Bader

Garden Folly and Estate Renovation, pages 86–99
    CONTRACTOR The Wills Company
    LANDSCAPE ARCHITECT Scott Byron & Co.
    INTERIOR DESIGN Whitney Baldwin
    PHOTOGRAPHER Witt Harmer

New-Fashioned Farmhouse, pages 100–115
    CONTRACTOR Marathon Construction Corp.
    LANDSCAPE ARCHITECT Scott Byron & Co.
    INTERIOR DESIGN Gaylynn E. Weaver
    PHOTOGRAPHER David Bader

Sprawling Shingle, pages 116–133
    CONTRACTOR Engerman Contracting
    LANDSCAPE ARCHITECT Scott Byron & Co.
    INTERIOR DESIGN Susan Kroeger, Ltd.
    PHOTOGRAPHER David Bader

Shingle Summerhouse, pages 134–149
    CONTRACTOR Moore Designs
    LANDSCAPE ARCHITECT Landworks
    INTERIOR DESIGN Jon Schlagenhaft
    PHOTOGRAPHER Wolfgang Weissmann and Matt Moran

Contemporary Folk, pages 150–167
    CONTRACTOR Castle Builders
    INTERIOR DESIGN Julie Couch Interiors; Mark Simmons
        Interiors; Rosanne Jackson for The Iron Gate
    PHOTOGRAPHER Alyssa Rosenheck

Cottage Romantic, pages 168–179
    CONTRACTOR Great Northern Construction
    LANDSCAPE ARCHITECT Scott Byron & Co.
    INTERIOR DESIGN Jose Carlino and Jennifer Schupie
        with Peabody's Interiors
    PHOTOGRAPHER Kaskel Photo

English Country Coastal, pages 180–191
    CONTRACTOR Moore Designs
    LANDSCAPE ARCHITECT Christina and David Plzak
    INTERIOR DESIGN Christina Plzak and Jennifer Schupie
    PHOTOGRAPHER David Bader

House for All Seasons, pages 192–203
    CONTRACTOR Moore Designs
    LANDSCAPE ARCHITECT Landworks
    INTERIOR DESIGN Jose Carlino and Jennifer Schupie of
        Peabody's Interiors
    PHOTOGRAPHER Doug Edmunds

North Shore Classic, pages 204–217
    CONTRACTOR Jeff Lynch Construction
    LANDSCAPE ARCHITECT Mariani Landscaping
    INTERIOR DESIGN Frank Ponterio Interior Design
    PHOTOGRAPHER David Bader

French Country House, pages 218–225
    CONTRACTOR Distinctive Custom Homes
    LANDSCAPE ARCHITECT ILT Vignocchi
    INTERIOR DESIGN Peabody's Interiors
    PHOTOGRAPHER David Bader

House on the Prairie, pages 226–233
    CONTRACTOR Sterling Hasey Co.
    LANDSCAPE ARCHITECT Flagstone Landscaping
    INTERIOR DESIGN Theresa Manns
    PHOTOGRAPHER David Bader

Urban Glamour, pages 234–247
    CONTRACTOR H. Findorff and Son, Inc.
    INTERIOR DESIGN Jon Schlagenhaft and Jessica
        Jubelirer
    PHOTOGRAPHER David Bader and Matt Moran

Erin Hills Golf Course, pages 248–259
    CONTRACTOR Ruvin Brothers
    LANDSCAPE ARCHITECT Landworks
    INTERIOR DESIGN Emily Winters of Peabody's Interiors
    PHOTOGRAPHER Unknown

German Equestrian Estate, pages 260–271
    CONTRACTOR Alfons Bruggehagen, AB-Bau
    LANDSCAPE ARCHITECT Udo Hollemann;
        Die Grünplaner
    INTERIOR DESIGN Michel Ceuterick
    PHOTOGRAPHER Unknown

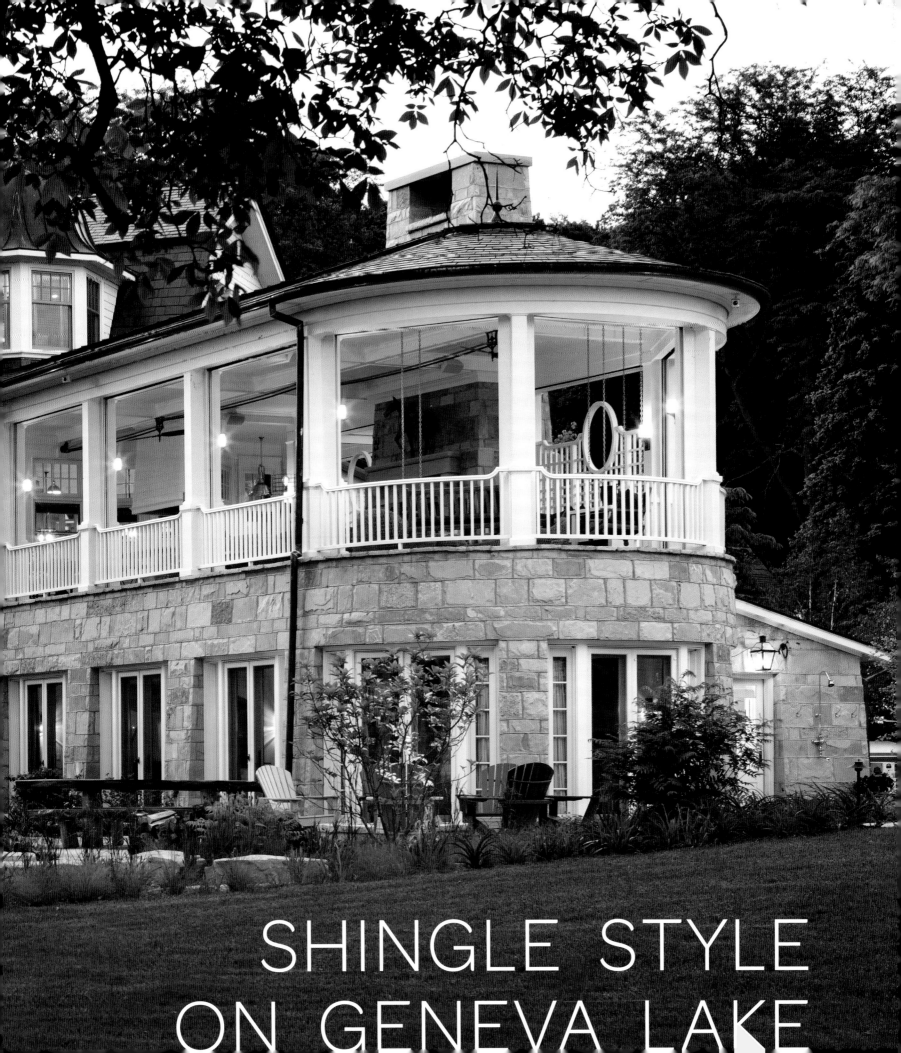

SHINGLE STYLE
ON GENEVA LAKE

A PORCH WITH PIZAZZ

The iconic American summer resort of Lake Geneva, Wisconsin, has its own eccentricities. Like its East Coast counterpart Newport, Rhode Island, this necklace of villages surrounding a large inland lake close to Chicago was born from the enormous wealth generated during the Industrial Age. Fortunes built from coal, oil, steel and railroads, along with lumber and livestock, were celebrated by lavish seasonal retreats. Fancy was viewed as good, as moguls tried to outdo each other with splendid houses and a high-style social order. Few live this way anymore, as elitism has been replaced by connectivity and an appreciation for relaxed elegance. But remnants of this giddy bygone era are evident in architecture—tiny bits of ornamentation and details that have no other purpose than to delight the eye.

For this house, inventive Shingle style was employed, albeit with a relaxed touch, mostly through curvaceous lines. Gambrel roofs, oval windows, arched openings and intricate balustrades abound in a house that practically dances across the landscape. Within, there are nooks, crannies, turrets, eaves and alcoves that add to the whimsical nature of the house, many expressed in evocative bead board, wainscoting and specialty tile.

The house's crowning glory is the veranda, extending off of one side like the prow of a Great Lakes steamship. With commanding views, it serves as an ideal venue for both large- and small-scale entertaining, offering shelter and shade while not denying a single speck of pleasure from the great outdoors.

Arched openings echo the dramatic vaulted ceilings, further emphasizing the geometry of the tiled floor inset. A roaring fireplace beckons one to "cozy up with a good book" in the definitive paneled study.

From the initial sketch, the expansive great room was designed to extend from the large kitchen opening. It offers flexible dining options via multiple tables, each seating eight guests comfortably. A built-in wood storage nook assures that the family won't have to go far to keep the fire crackling warm.

The light-flooded kitchen is punctuated by a cozy wraparound breakfast nook. Polished nickel hardware along with a rolling library ladder bring English country house grandeur to the finished composition.

The stair hall is both expansive and welcoming, with masterful millwork throughout. Multipaned transoms, which keep openings to a comfortable scale but allow light to penetrate between rooms, are thematic throughout the entire house.

At the top of the stairs, a conversation landing is dressed for the
occasion with whimsical balloon chairs.

Bead board encircles the bedroom ceiling, while bell-curved moldings lift the space in a soft and gentle manner in this master bedroom.

The intricate, dark tile walls create a glossy texture and pattern in the master bath. The tub is nestled into a light-filled dormer, where the view can be enjoyed while soaking.

The lower level gathering space is a family-friendly area for entertaining. The French doors arranged around the curve open out to the pool and fire pit area.

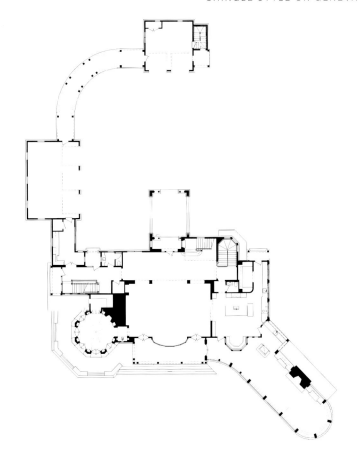

CABIN
RETREATS

UP NORTH AUTHENTIC

In the Midwest, "Up North" refers to not just a geographical location but a way of life. As far removed from anything urban as humanly possible, regardless of the actual distance, it is a mind-set embedded in a culture that embraces nature. For generations, people have seen the value of dialing back their lives and replacing all things tame and polished with the raw and wild for a season.

This aesthetic is especially robust in the northernmost reaches of Wisconsin, Michigan and Minnesota, where wildlife abounds and mirror-perfect lakes dot verdant forests. Here, on the banks of one such lake, was a timeworn fishing resort—an authentic "camp" waiting to be awakened for yet another generation.

The existing cabins served as the template for the camp's new incarnation. Three structures were restored, rebuilt and reconfigured, while also being discreetly outfitted with every contemporary comfort. A consistent vocabulary of river rock, timber and golden knotty pine was engaged for authenticity. Inside and out, classic Adirondack details were used to seamlessly create a serenely rustic attitude. By day, the structures recede into the surrounding woods, their spacious porches serving as picture frames for the expansive views. But by night, the interiors positively glow with cozy warmth.

Surrounding grounds were landscaped with a decidedly gentle touch. Nothing appears too new or deliberate, allowing the woods, water and sky to take center stage. Regardless of the season, from snowbound winters to shimmering summers, Mother Nature is definitely the star of this show.

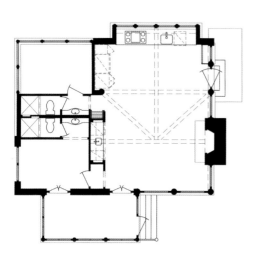

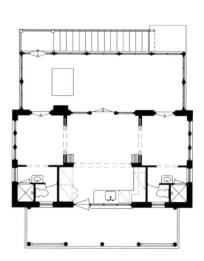

The byword is *cozy,* regardless of the season. Interiors are kept functionally casual, in the spirit of the camp aesthetic.

Polished log rafters and beams are contrasted by the textured rubble stone fireplace.

The open kitchen caters to conversation and shared time with family and friends. Tucked around the corner is a large, open-shelved pantry, so the house is always stocked for a crowd.

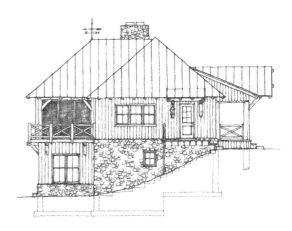

For this idyllic cabin, the screened porch overlooking the sparkling lake is the heart and soul of the house. Furnishings are eclectic, with touches of camp kitsch and classic Native American motifs.

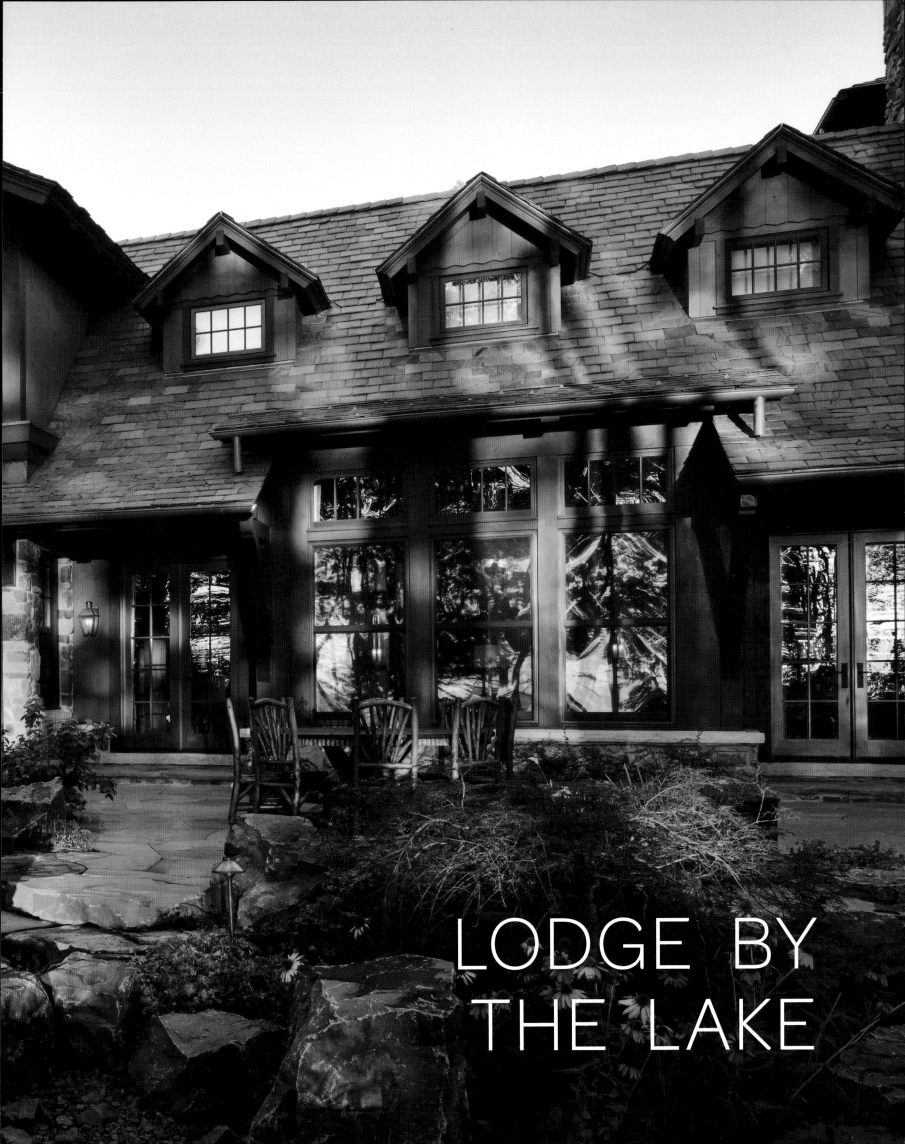

LODGE BY
THE LAKE

A MIDWESTERN MOUNTAIN MANOR

Architecture is at its best when it is at one with the environment, and climate plays a pivotal role in defining that aspect. The Midwest is unique in that it is home to a climate featuring sharp contrasts between classically cold and snowy winters and languid summers, with gentle springs and yawning autumns being dauntingly brief. Too, rather than a progressive fade from one season to the next, there are foreshocks of what's to come followed by a return to what was. For this reason, houses in this region demand a concerted effort to be adaptive at a moment's notice. The surprise bonus, however, is that houses aren't as tightly programmed as they might be elsewhere.

The densely forested bluffs and deep ravines that hug the shores of Lake Michigan are an unexpected sight to first-time visitors who expect nothing more than plain prairie flatness from the Midwestern states. But this dramatic terrain most certainly exists, with all of the evocative majesty one normally associates with locales on Mountain Time.

Here, the rustic, bold vocabulary of rough-cut stone and substantial timber could not be more appropriate. By employing the aesthetic of heavily extended eaves and a decided heft to the base of the structure, with a dry moat entrance, the end result is a jubilant expression of classic mountain lodge style, albeit deluxe. The slate and copper roof adds to the authenticity of a house designed to feel as though it grew up and out of the surrounding forest. *Painterly* would be an appropriate adjective.

Within, the house possesses every modern expectation, with soaring rooms and an open plan perfectly planned for entertaining on any scale. Of course, the many fireplaces serve as both focal points and cozy perches for cold-weather gatherings. And when a crackling fire isn't quite enough to cut the chill in the evening air, the in-ground hot tub beckons.

Throughout, views across the house and out into the natural landscape were given the highest priority. Each and every detail — from positioning to structure to materials — was carefully considered, just as a frame maker would do for an important painting.

Heavy timbers distinguish the soaring great room, while a catwalk on the second floor overlooks the space, providing a discreet observation point ever so slightly removed from the activities below.

Above all else, this is a house for entertaining, as evidenced by the many spaces and features for gracious hospitality.

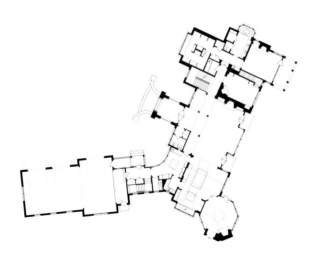

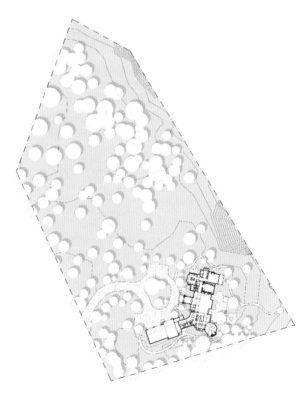

Typically, for most social gatherings the kitchen serves as a magnet to both hosts and guests. A pair of islands provide ample surfaces for meal preparation, as well as abundant gathering spaces for family and friends.

A horseshoe bar serves as the focal point for the in-home cocktail lounge. Towering illuminated shelves display a passionate collection of craft spirits.

The dry moat around the front entrance seems perfectly suited to the house's stately facade. Bellcast eaves and a flared, arched portico add to the otherworldly charm.

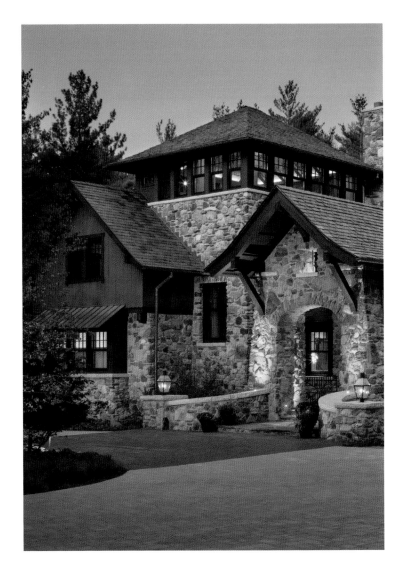

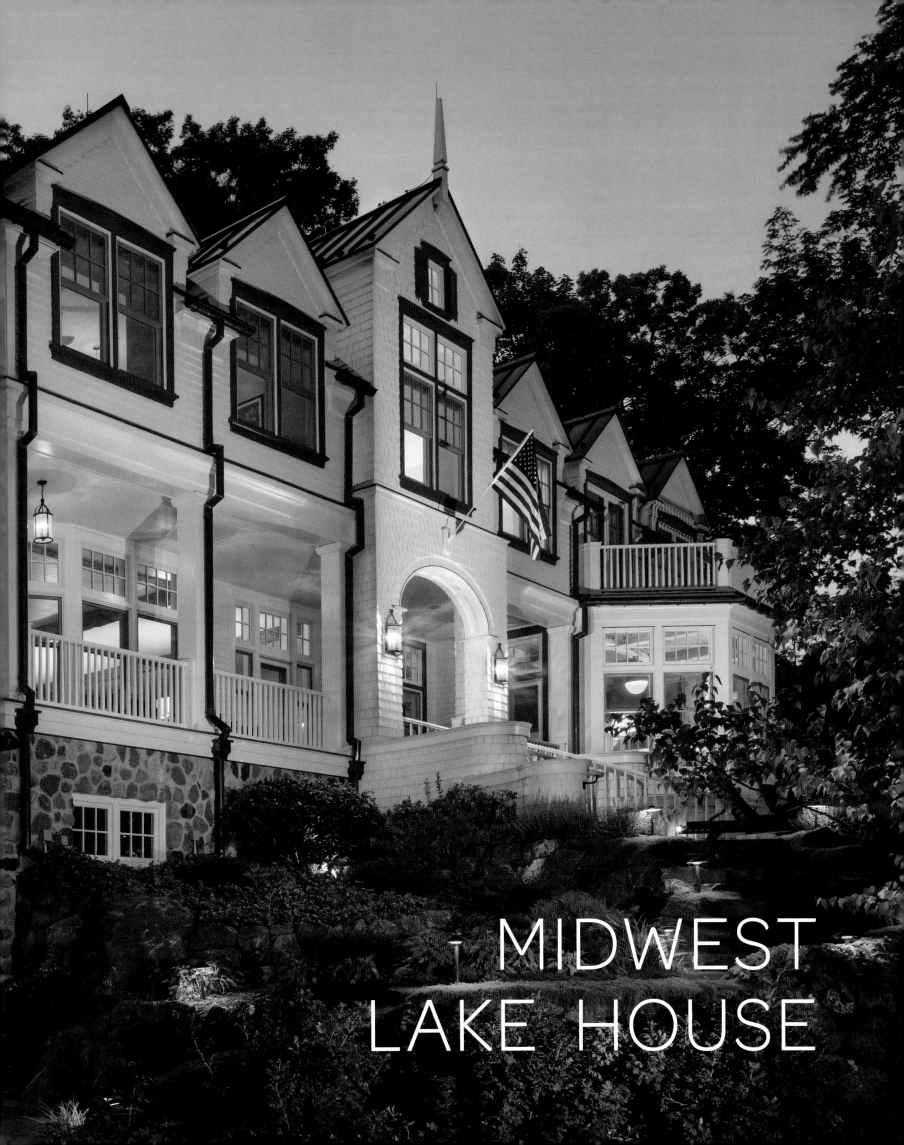

MIDWEST
LAKE HOUSE

BOATHOUSE BEGINNINGS

Every heirloom house begins with a passion, and for this gracious getaway on Big Cedar Lake, it was competitive rowing. The homeowners had a tremendous affinity for not only the sport, as they were former Olympians, but also the stylistic trappings of a pursuit so saturated with lyrical beauty that it has inspired painters and other creative expressionists since its earliest days. The first rowing club in the United States was the Detroit Boat Club, founded in 1839. In 1852, the first actual recorded race was between Harvard and Yale, and the rest is history.

The mystique of rowing centers on the interaction between water, wood and muscle. Add to that the evocative nature of boathouses, where all of these elements need to converse in the language of architecture, and you have the germ of a design that incorporates the highly decorative exuberance of the Victorian era with aspects of the humble utility buildings typical of the Midwestern countryside. The exposed foundation, made solely of local sand, cement and split fieldstone, provides both a physical and emotional sense of place on which this grand lake house, with its soaring interiors and deftly detailed facade, stands tall for the sheer pleasure of it all.

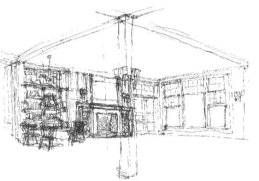

Shiplap ceilings echo the boathouse aesthetic of the entire structure. The substantial newel and finial delightfully contrast with the delicacy of the staircase spindles, making them appear even more ethereal.

While the material elements of the house's vocabulary are completely traditional, the floor plan is open, allowing for optimal flexibility and flow. No space is too tightly programmed.

A mudroom is a fixture of family living. Here, it is given ample attention with thoughtful cabinetry. A distinctive rustic fireplace is inset into a wall of reclaimed wood.

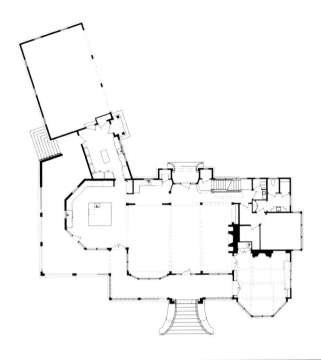

The lateral fireplace and fieldstone surround provide a muscular edge to an otherwise gentle bedroom.
The unique ceiling profile reveals the complexities of the house's roofline.

Smooth river rocks form the floor of a glass-enclosed shower, bringing the feel of the outdoors in. Intricate, strongly geometric tile work on both the shower walls and the bathroom floor add visual punch.

The lyrical watercolor and pencil rendering of
the house reflects its gentle spirit perfectly.

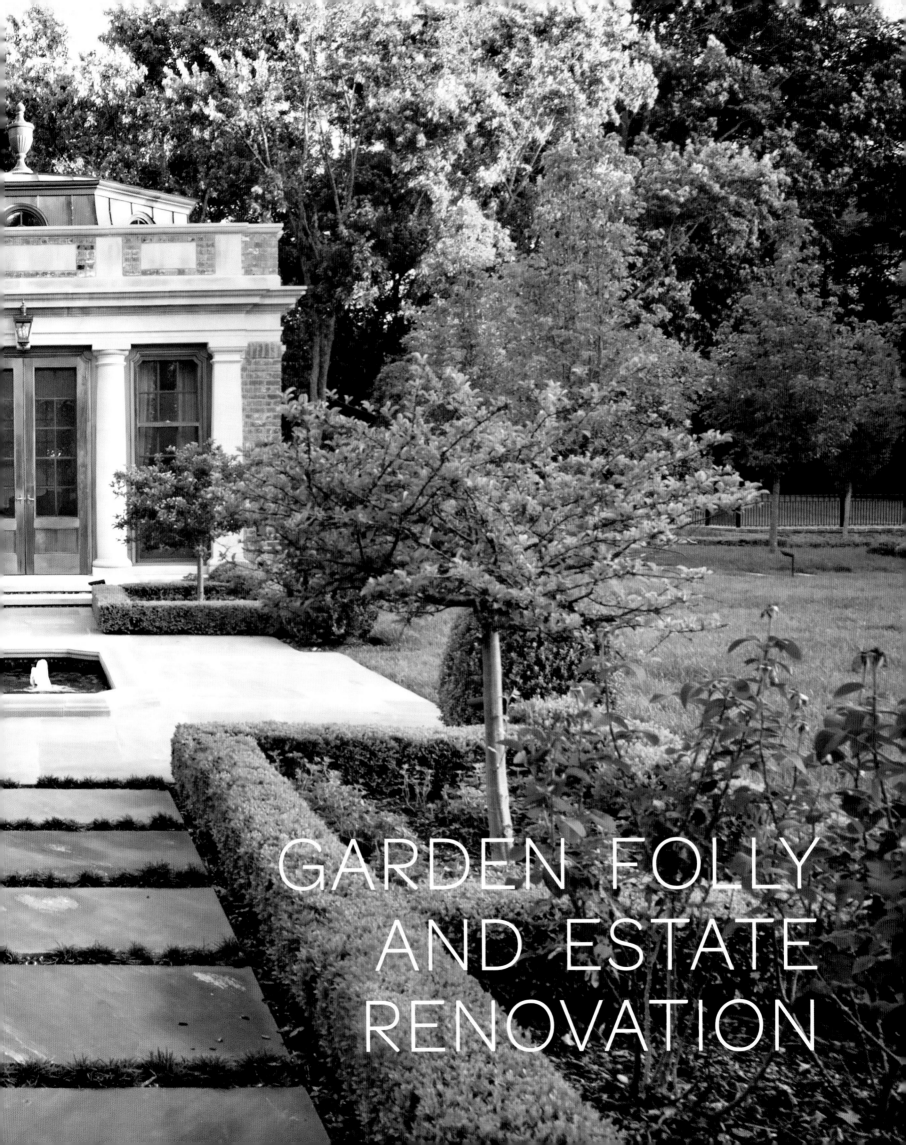

GARDEN FOLLY
AND ESTATE
RENOVATION

ICING ON THE CAKE

Once upon a time, in one of Nashville's most prominent historic neighborhoods, there lived a stately house of brick and stone that could not be more quintessentially Georgian in style and gentle in its siting on a picturesque, tree-lined street. Changes in lifestyle over time, however, along with the dreams of the house's owners to host large-scale social gatherings, inspired a fresh perspective that fulfilled these dreams while at all times being respectful to the "architectural correctness" of the existing house. This being the South, any modifications and additions had to be done with a watchful eye to the essence of gracious hospitality. This was, indeed, a labor of love.

Less-than-wonderful additions and renovations that had been built over the years were either removed or restyled, and a gracious outdoor dining terrace was defined. A large covered porch with an outdoor fireplace and even more dining and relaxing options was built, along with a glamorous pool and patio.

But, then, there's the big surprise: a spectacular architectural folly was designed, not only to delight the eye but also to serve as a true four-seasons entertaining destination. Inspired by classical French and English design, what it lacks in square footage is compensated for by exuberant interior and exterior detailing. Programmed to service poolside activities (it houses a well-appointed bar), it couldn't be further from the traditional concept of a cabana. Rather, it is an exercise in the thoughtful use of exquisite materials and applications—from its character-grade maple ceiling to the intricately carved stone fireplace and deluxe furnishings—that just happens to be by the pool.

Pencil drawings illustrate the views around the property and how the new structures will integrate seamlessly into what exists. A sectional perspective of the folly reveals the breathtaking artistry of the roofline.

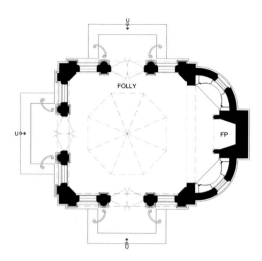

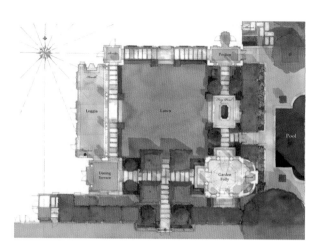

With so much detail involved in the scheme, symmetry becomes an important element in bringing harmony to the overall composition.

The family commissioned a scale model of the folly, which provides a different vantage point of this detailed structure.

The rear facade of the folly is left intentionally soft-spoken to allow for a gentle transition to the pool terrace. Greenery artfully climbs the exterior of the chimney wall.

A soft white paint color is blended with touches of pale gray stone, wood, wicker and distressed copper for a completely organic statement.

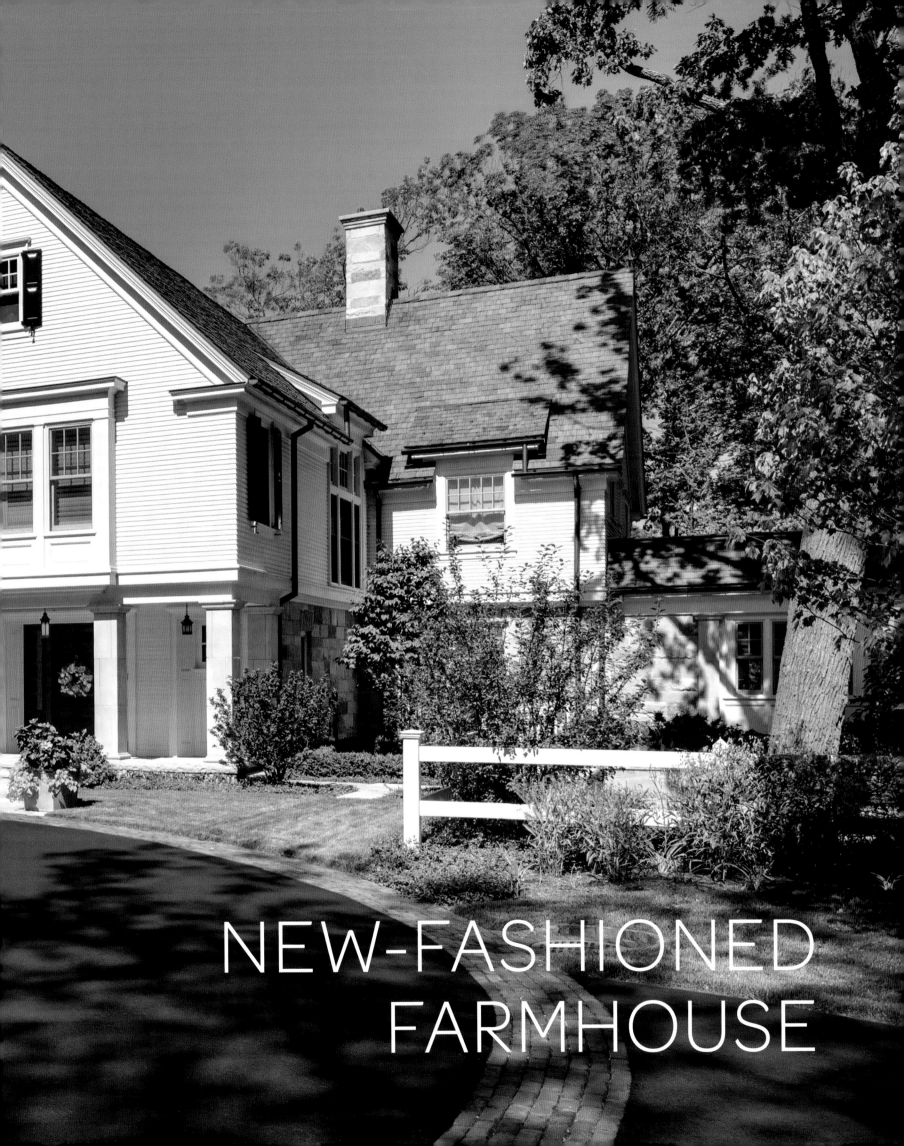

NEW-FASHIONED
FARMHOUSE

BUILT TO LAST

The American family house has undergone some pretty extraordinary changes in the past few decades. Gone are the days of the typical center-hall colonial with its standard arrangement of tightly programmed rooms. Like life itself, impacted by gigantic leaps in technology and the relaxing of longstanding social mores, everything today is so much more fluid. The traditional living room has become passé; kitchens are now required to be multifunctional and have grown to proportions that typically include what used to be called the family room; and baths have evolved into the realm of spa-like luxury.

Stainless steel, granite, artisanal stone, ceramic and glass are now commonplace, and a soaring entrance hall is de rigueur, even in what used to be referred to as "starter house" neighborhoods, where practically every house is exactly the same as the one next door.

However, for those with the means for a truly bespoke family house, an entirely new concept has emerged: the imposing but lyrical structure, one with an exterior that appears as though it could have been built decades ago but with an interior that could not be more of-the-moment. This is such a house, employing traditional materials and the highest levels of craftsmanship, all delicately and sensitively tailored to ensure balance and harmony, especially important given the location—a distinguished row of grand historic houses on stately properties hugging the shore of Lake Michigan.

An imposing projection is centered on the central structure, allowing for a broad and gracious front porch. Enclosed breezeways extend from each side, connecting to completely stone-clad twin wings.

Within, the house unfolds, revealing alluring vistas that are almost universally warmed by the southern sun. Arched openings are a unifying theme, detailed in simple but perfectly articulated millwork. Ceiling heights, while certainly not cramped, were intentionally kept more traditionally scaled for both comfort and ambience. Rooms flow into each other—big where they needed to be big, such as the combined kitchen and family room, but also with intimate spaces for quiet conversation. Old-fashioned elements like pocket doors and gentle barrel-vaulted ceilings were employed for charm. The site, which originally featured an unbroken gentle slope, was excavated to allow for a completely functional, light-filled lower level overlooking a stony ravine, finished with an in-ground hot tub, weather permitting, while also serving as a buffer against cold winter winds.

While this is indeed a house of considerable size with plenty of room for large gatherings of family and friends, it remains cozy and comfortable, warm and inviting—the perfect place to bring up a brood.

The floor plan of the house echoes the balance of the mature trees that surround the structure.

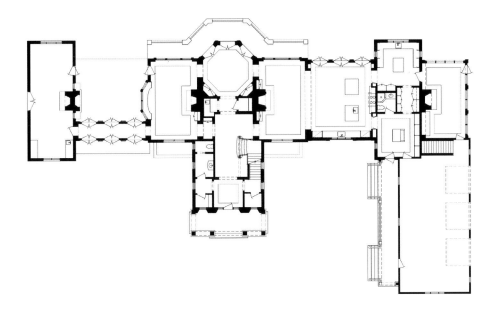

Generously extended archways provide the ease of a contemporary
open plan while maintaining a decidedly traditional feel.

An artfully vaulted ceiling in the kitchen repeats the theme of gentle curves that runs throughout the house.

Large, ganged, double-hung windows maintain the charming farmhouse feel of a bedroom, even when the view outside is spectacular. Staircases, too, are treated simply to support the essential aura of humility.

The master bath and adjoining dressing room feature the warmth of wide-plank wooden floors, also providing needed softness against the generous use of marble.

The lake-front dining porch is embellished with a chunky stone fireplace and extended hearth, along with a built-in barbecue station for substantial alfresco meals.

SPRAWLING
SHINGLE

SIMPLE PLEASURE

In architecture, simplicity is a virtue; but it requires the same attention to detail and integrity of materials that more ornate structures typically demand. When design elements are pared down to basics, every little bit counts. Such was the philosophy applied to this sprawling Shingle-style home—a gentle giant composed of natural cedar shakes, local stone, copper, glass and a fair amount of white paint. "I believe in optimism and plenty of white paint!" said the decor oracle Elsie de Wolfe, whose belief that a proper house should be delightfully airy and open rather than insular and intimidating impacted residential design in ways that we all take for granted today.

Like so many Midwestern houses that enjoy lake-front siting, this house endeavors to make the most of dramatic water views and precious sunshine. In response to proximate neighboring houses, a shallow, almost semicircular, terrain-hugging floor plan was employed to allow southern light to penetrate every room and create a central enclosure for subtle privacy. The house truly embraces, while remaining breezy and accessible.

Taking the Midwestern potpourri of weather extremes into account, over-hangs were intentionally made generous to allow for open windows during even the most relentless rainstorms, while rooflines were built with expansive slopes for optimal snow shedding. This is a house that wears its structural elements proudly, with exposed beaming and a total lack of pretension. Every element is there for a reason, creating a house that delivers the message of common sense and easy comfort.

The modified butterfly floor plan embraces the terrain while also framing the sweeping lake-front vista. The bonus is the creation of a protected patio for outdoor dining.

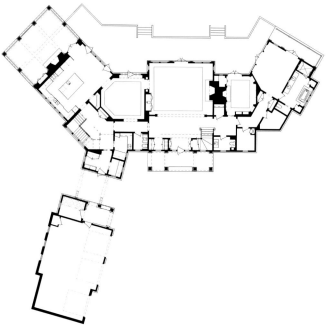

A cozy paneled library provides the perfect getaway space.

The spa-like bath features discreet accents of palest aqua and sea glass green.

A large veranda could not be more functional, with multiple seating areas for conversation and dining along with a generous fieldstone fireplace.

SHINGLE SUMMERHOUSE

THE ALLURE OF THE LAKE

Midwest lakeside life has its own style. There is a sweet, homespun charm, even in the face of an influx of large, sophisticated houses. But by injecting the humble aesthetics of the American farmhouse—once the norm for this neck of the woods—with the decorative elements in vogue when the majority of the settlement of the Midwest as we know it began, a delightfully appropriate house is achievable, one that respects its location while successfully serving the needs and expectations of modern life.

For this grand weekend getaway that needed to accommodate multiple generations, a classic Shingle-style vernacular was the sensible choice. The house has decided personality, but in typical Midwestern fashion, it is soft-spoken. The facade is deceptively plain, with a simple columned entrance porch. But inside the front door, spirited exuberance takes over. A wide staircase ascending to the second floor boasts a finely detailed banister that turns to form an oval-framed view of the rafters. Curvilinear motifs continue, from the rounded shape of the exquisite gathering room to the elegantly arched eyebrow dormers.

The house features a huge hub kitchen with adjacent pantries and scullery, making it the perfect gathering place not just for meals but for activities of all kinds. An attached gazebo, porch with phantom screens that disappear at the touch of a button, and almost grade-level verandas dot the lake side of the house. Beyond, an expansive lawn slopes towards the shoreline, creating the essential connection between house and water that is part and parcel to a proper Midwestern lakeside residence.

A circular theme radiates throughout the entire house, from room shapes to window details to an extraordinary custom rug that anchors the oval great room.

The large kitchen features three distinct areas for meal preparation, dining, and lounging — all without walls but clearly programmed and perfect for large family gatherings.

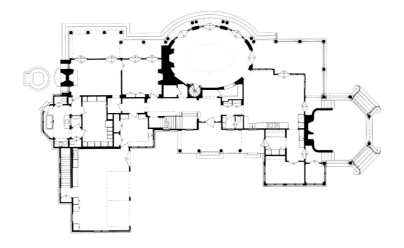

A freestanding soaking tub is tucked into its own arched alcove featuring a large bay window.

A wine cellar provides a quiet spot for tasting and conversation, while a screened porch with electric screens hosts more exuberant activities. A widow's walk extends off the loft of the game room inside the house.

CONTEMPORARY FOLK

LOCAL COLOR

Creating a house that speaks to its locale, one that celebrates tradition and terrain with graceful familiarity, is part and parcel to an architect's task. Here, a new house was constructed with a heavy dose of Southern charm, respectful of the indigenous stylings of the Nashville aesthetic while uncompromising in its relevance.

An expansive, welcoming front porch, essential for the rigors of a hot, humid climate, leads to a colonial-inspired central entry. Within, a gently sweeping grand staircase harkens back to the era of rustling skirts and copious petticoats, but that's where the nostalgia ends. A contemporary open plan could not be more of-the-moment, with large, soaring rooms that effortlessly flow into one another, in keeping with how modern families actually live.

As airy and luminous as the house is, it needed a buffer to shield it from exposure to an adjacent road. A service and garage wing was built for that purpose, which also helped to define a two-sided courtyard for outdoor entertaining, complete with fireplace. Details were carefully edited and intentionally minimized to suit the vernacular of the well-mannered, simple pleasures of a good old Southern house.

This Nashville farmhouse, which includes a wide, welcoming veranda and twin chimneys, gives a completely new house permission to coexist with its neighbors harmoniously. The gently curving entry drive opens up to an ample motor court.

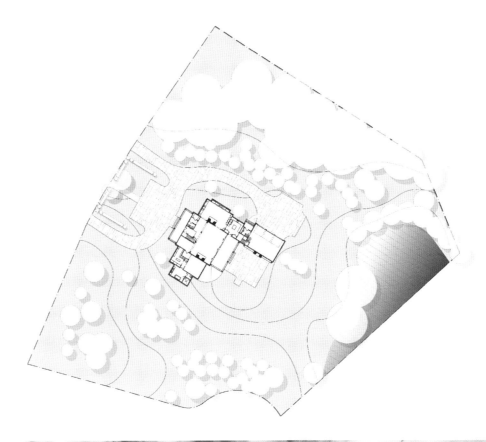

The great room is open and casual, with one entire side lined with French doors leading out to the rear yard.

All cabinetry is designed to meld with the house's architecture, creating unbroken lines for maximum volume. The dramatic staircase is purposefully exposed, bringing a sculptural element into the entire great room.

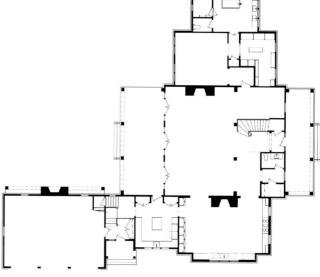

An oversized island does double duty for meal preparation and casual dining. A pair of wrought iron lanterns lift the eye, furthering the soaring nature of the double-height kitchen.

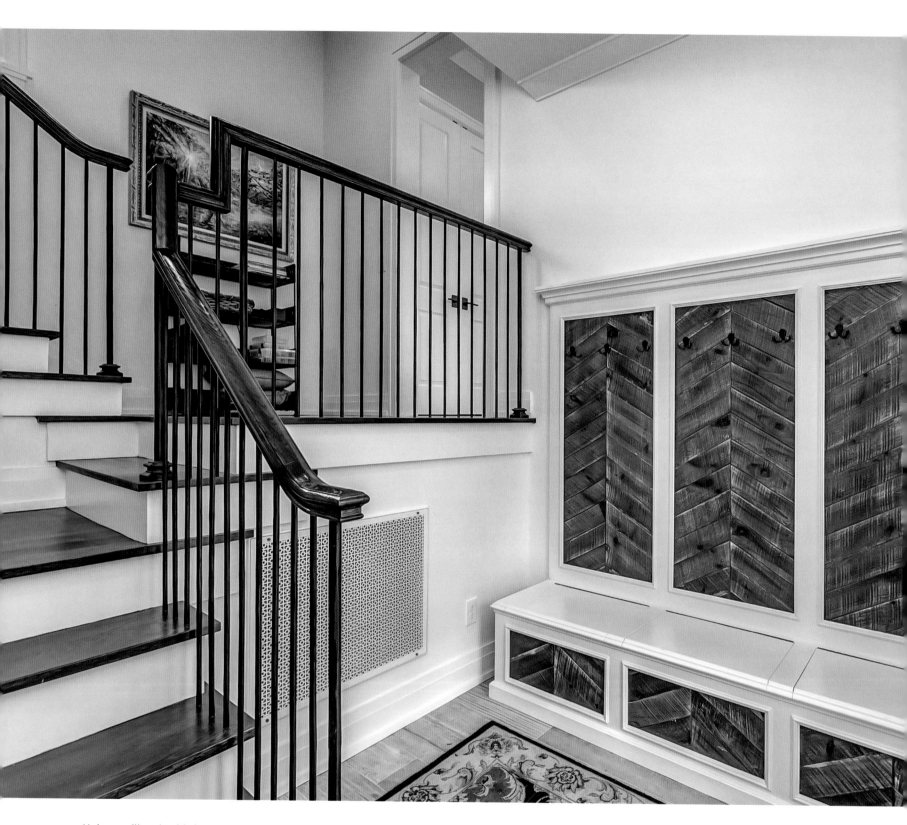

Unique millwork adds interest, such as the application of rough-hewn boards in a herringbone pattern for a coat and boot station at the foot of the stairs.

The light-filled bath suggests a classic sunporch, with vanity mirrors cleverly suspended in front of the windows.

An alfresco living room is formed in the courtyard by grouping furniture around an outdoor fireplace. The large lantern further defines the space. Generous sheltered wood piles become sculptural elements.

COTTAGE
ROMANTIC

THE AUDACITY OF AUTHENTIC

Door County, a peninsula extending into Lake Michigan, is nicknamed "The Cape Cod of the Midwest." Like its eastern counterpart, there are two distinct sides: the northwestern shore, which meanders along sparkling Green Bay—a yachtsman's paradise—and the southeastern shore, which fronts the mesmerizing vastness of Lake Michigan. Dotted along both shorelines are charming towns, each with its own personality.

The centrally located town of Fish Creek, on Green Bay, was the first to attract the smart set, particularly wealthy industrial families from Chicago and Milwaukee. On an especially breathtaking bluff is Cottage Row, home to many magnificent lake-style houses built at the beginning of the twentieth century. Redbird Manor is one of them—an authentic Jazz Age retreat.

Sadly neglected for far too long, the house and its outbuildings were in bad shape. Wood had rotted, windows were failing and the porch had collapsed. Yet rather than tear it down and start from scratch, the owners embarked on a courageous two-and-a-half-year restoration. What was usable was carefully removed and refinished; what wasn't, was faithfully reproduced. The end result is a magically luminous house firmly rooted in its evocative past but perfectly poised for the future.

The owners desired a home in which "to celebrate, study, ponder big-life decisions, and sometimes just reacquaint yourself with who you are." Indeed, they received that and so much more. Interior and exterior paints were custom blended to match the house's original colors, and family heirlooms were carefully integrated with new furnishings that were curated for comfort and timelessness. "Meaningful bits and pieces from long ago quietly grace every room," says one of the owners. And there, atop a gentle rise of verdant lawn at water's edge, a much-loved old lake house lives on for generations to come.

The same local stone that was used for exterior elements such as retaining walls and door surrounds reappears indoors for the charmingly scaled chimney.

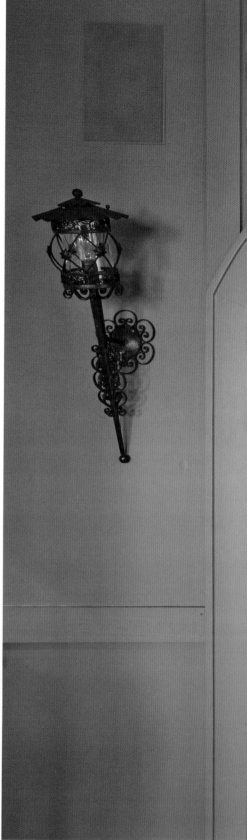

A unique turquoise paint color adds an element of eclecticism to the main living area.

Little details such as octagonal windows and artful knotty-pine millwork provide personality in even the smallest spaces, such as this tucked away powder room.

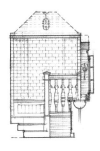
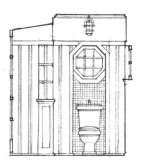
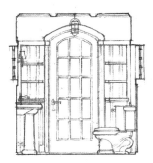

The sunny enclosed porch is almost completely lined in bead board, save for the stone chimney and nostalgic checkerboard floor.

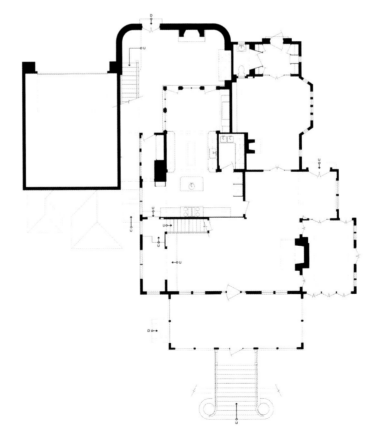

ENGLISH COUNTRY
COASTAL

A FAMILY HOME WITH AN ENGLISH ACCENT

The half-timbered house has been around since Medieval times, yet it continues to be one of the most beloved residential architectural styles. Beams, cross beams and braces are exposed, with the spaces between the timbers typically filled with stucco, brick or stone, many times in combination. It is this artful mix of materials that allows for unique compositions. But the real bonus of this style of construction is the ability to deftly control mass: big houses don't loom, and small houses are given beguiling charm.

Usually associated with the romantic English countryside, this glorious aesthetic began to make regular appearances in the leafy suburbs of 1920s America. In this gentle giant of a storybook house, it feels as though time has stopped. Warm wood is everywhere, bringing the outdoors in and creating a lyrical habitat for happy family living. A soaring two-story central hall crowned by a library loft is both baronial and conducive to connectivity: one can get a sense of nearly every room in the house from a single vantage point.

By day, the structure recedes into the landscape, gracefully melding with surrounding trees and lawn and sky. By night, light dances from every pane of glass in the most dramatic fashion, made all the more magical and mysterious by the home's many nooks and crannies, eaves, peaks and dormers.

Regardless of the season, the house maintains a timeless, storybook attitude that recalls the romanticism of a Currier & Ives engraving.

© 2009 Wade Weissmann Architecture Inc.

Richly stained window casings, paneling and flooring create an overwhelmingly cozy feel.

A consistent architectural vocabulary was desired throughout the house, including the kitchen. A light-colored island enlivens the space.

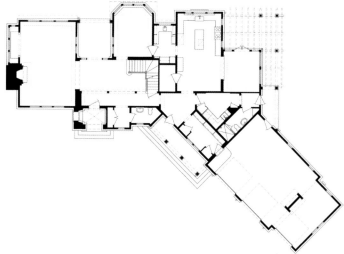

191

The second-story sitting area is given loft-like appeal with beautifully articulated beaming. A large fireplace with decorative tile surround anchors the room.

HOUSE FOR
ALL SEASONS

MAXIMIZED POTENTIAL

Houses rarely end up exactly where they started, except for the few that are either so extraordinary or historically significant that we don't dare alter them. Rather, houses evolve in response to societal changes, developments in technology and, as we are seeing in our own lifetime, changes in climate. The economics of a region can shrink or expand, affecting not only the demand for housing but also the kind of housing demanded by the surrounding population.

When the owners purchased this house, they recognized that it would need to be renovated; the spaces just weren't appropriate to their lifestyle. So they embarked on a plan to make the existing house absolutely the best it could be. The interior was completely gutted and reconfigured, while the exterior was redressed, adding design integrity and historical accuracy. In keeping with contemporary tastes for generous rooms, all ceiling heights were raised, resulting in increased light and grander proportions.

Connected by a sunlit semicircular gallery, a new pavilion was built for entertaining. It houses a library, home theater and screened porch. An imposing octagonal great room is clad almost entirely in reclaimed wood, providing a stunning space for large gatherings while truly blurring the lines between indoors and out, as the house is situated in a clearing surrounded by mature trees.

The finishing touch was to reengineer adjoining wetlands to create a serene pond, providing an ever-changing vista that attracts wildlife and catches the sunlight in beguiling ways. By building on what was there, celebrating what was good and addressing what wasn't, a good house was given the chance to soar to new heights.

A wet bar gives functional appeal to the transitional space leading to the octagonal great room.

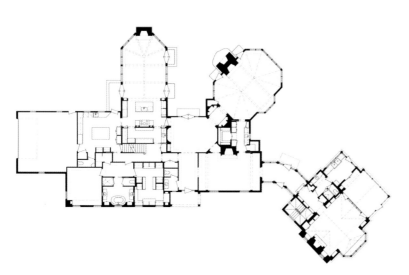

Uniquely shaped rooms, punctuated with bays, fireplaces, and shaped ceilings, add interest in multiple dimensions throughout this house.

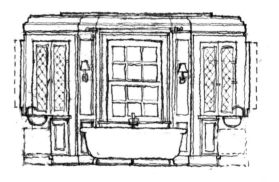

All baths are finely detailed. Traditionally styled cabinetry and fixtures tucked into arched or rounded niches complete the custom look.

NORTH SHORE
CLASSIC

EMPTY NESTERS' PARADISE

For a lively couple desiring a home for their newly downsized life, there was a definite wish list. Admirers of French Norman architecture, they wanted a residence that was substantial, distinguished and able to host large gatherings of family and friends. But they also wanted a cozy retreat in which they would not feel lost. The solution was a two-pronged design. One side provides an expansive gathering room that flows seamlessly into the kitchen, dining room and screened porch. On the opposite side of the house, far removed from the public spaces, are an intimate library, master bedroom and bath, carefully arranged as a totally private suite of rooms. On the lower level is the ultimate unexpected amenity—a dodgeball room for the family to play their favorite game.

The whole is brought together through an artful combination of brick, slate, copper, timber and stone, used both indoors and out with gusto, for a jewel box of a country manor house that's built for two or two hundred.

The house abounds with romantic, painterly details such as turrets, cupolas, arched openings and insets of grillwork. The stone-quoined exterior elevations are echoed in masterful paneling within.

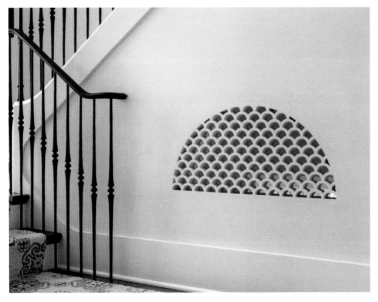

Rooms flow into one another with easy grace, providing for flexible entertaining. A reclaimed wood ceiling in the great room keeps all formality at bay.

The exuberant kitchen is both theatrical and functional, turning even the simplest of meals into special occasions.

An intimate library provides a quiet retreat. Clever pivoting shelves reveal themselves as discreet doors when privacy is desired.

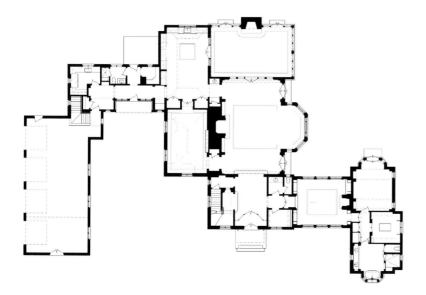

Curvaceous elements appear throughout the house, from arched recesses to windows to dramatically vaulted ceilings. At the back of the house, a large loggia serves as a bridge between the interior spaces and the expansive grounds.

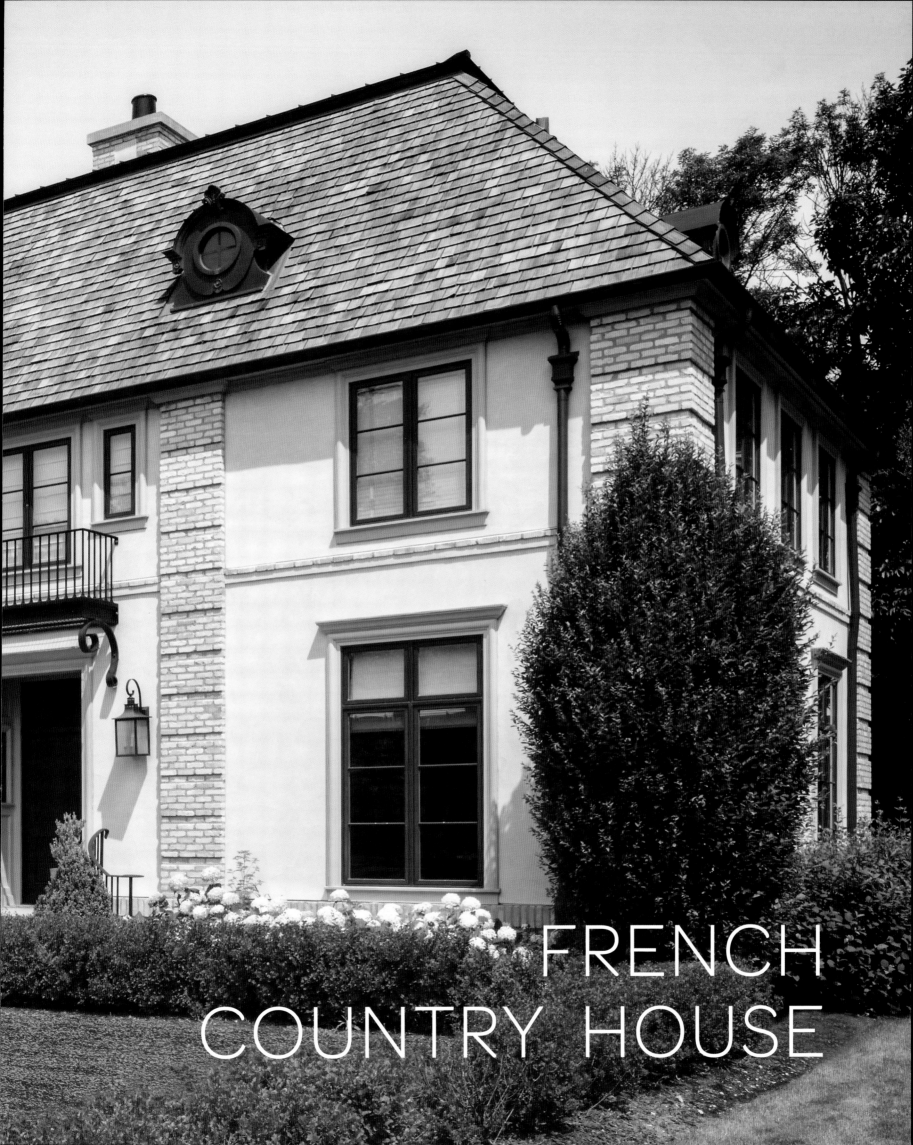

FRENCH
COUNTRY HOUSE

FRENCH PARADOX

Often, a client dreams of living in one house while actually needing another for their lifestyle. This was the case for a vibrant family that desired a home that could function in multiple situations. They admired historic European estate houses built in another era, with structure, majesty and a decided sense of permanence. But they also wanted to live in the now, with spaces that could easily transition from formal to fun.

This stately French Norman manor in the Chicago suburb of Lake Forest was designed with the family's perspective in mind, along with a nod towards timeless elegance. The formal facade belies a delightful, light-filled interior, with a soaring entry and a contemporary open plan. Rooms flow into one another with youthful ease and not the slightest tinge of rigid formality, illustrating how generous spaces can also be surprisingly cozy.

Siting was critical. The house was placed squarely in the middle of the property, creating four distinct quadrants for outdoor living, including a garden and a south-facing orchard.

Rather than the traditional arrangement of rooms radiating off of a central hallway, the layout was simplified for fewer defined spaces and a relaxed flow. This arrangement allows for even the north-facing rooms to benefit from southern light coming from the adjacent space, a decided bonus in a region where winters can be bleak. The end result is a happy house that is both distinguished and loaded with ample *joie de vivre*.

An alfresco dining terrace is detailed as distinctively as if it were an interior space. The outdoor fireplace features a limestone mantel over which a chamfered corner inset is formed by the chimney brickwork. Within, the house's serpentine staircase sets a lyrical tone.

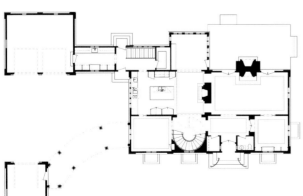

HOUSE ON
THE PRAIRIE

THE CHARM OF THE FARM

For centuries, the American farmhouse has been an integral part of a seemingly unending architectural conversation. Born out of necessity as basic shelter for those seeking to work the land, it was never a style but rather a response to whatever humble materials were available, along with the demands of the particular climate and terrain. Yet the aesthetic of the farmhouse—plain lines, an overall lack of ornamentation or color and purely functional construction—could not be more stylish. A case in point would be this seemingly simple house built into a gentle slope of the Wisconsin prairie. At first blush it seems composed of a single long, low, shed-like building flanked by two smaller support structures. A tractor wouldn't appear out of place, nor would a rusty pickup truck.

But in reality, this is a sophisticated home for worldly owners. The main interior space surprises with its lofty, exposed-beam airiness. Dark floors and generous dark-framed windows punctuate the space, which is outfitted in an eclectic mix of midcentury modern furnishings. Beyond, an enticing porch blurs the lines between indoors and out, as three large openings along the room have neither windows nor doors. But at the touch of a button, screens magically descend from hidden recesses.

The ultimate surprise is on the lower level: no common dank basement, this. Where one would expect to find the workman-like aspects of a house—maybe just a furnace, a water heater and a washtub—is a classic car collector's paradise, a garage of such pristine perfection that it could easily serve as a party space. And in keeping with the owners' passion for horsepower, the grounds adjacent to the house have a beautifully crafted corral, a most fitting hangout for the family steed.

A dramatic stepped fireplace serves as both a strong architectural element and a room divider, creating a cozy home office and library behind it. Millwork echoes the stone's muted tones, with dramatic cerulean accents.

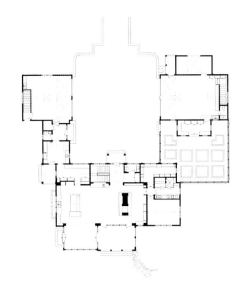

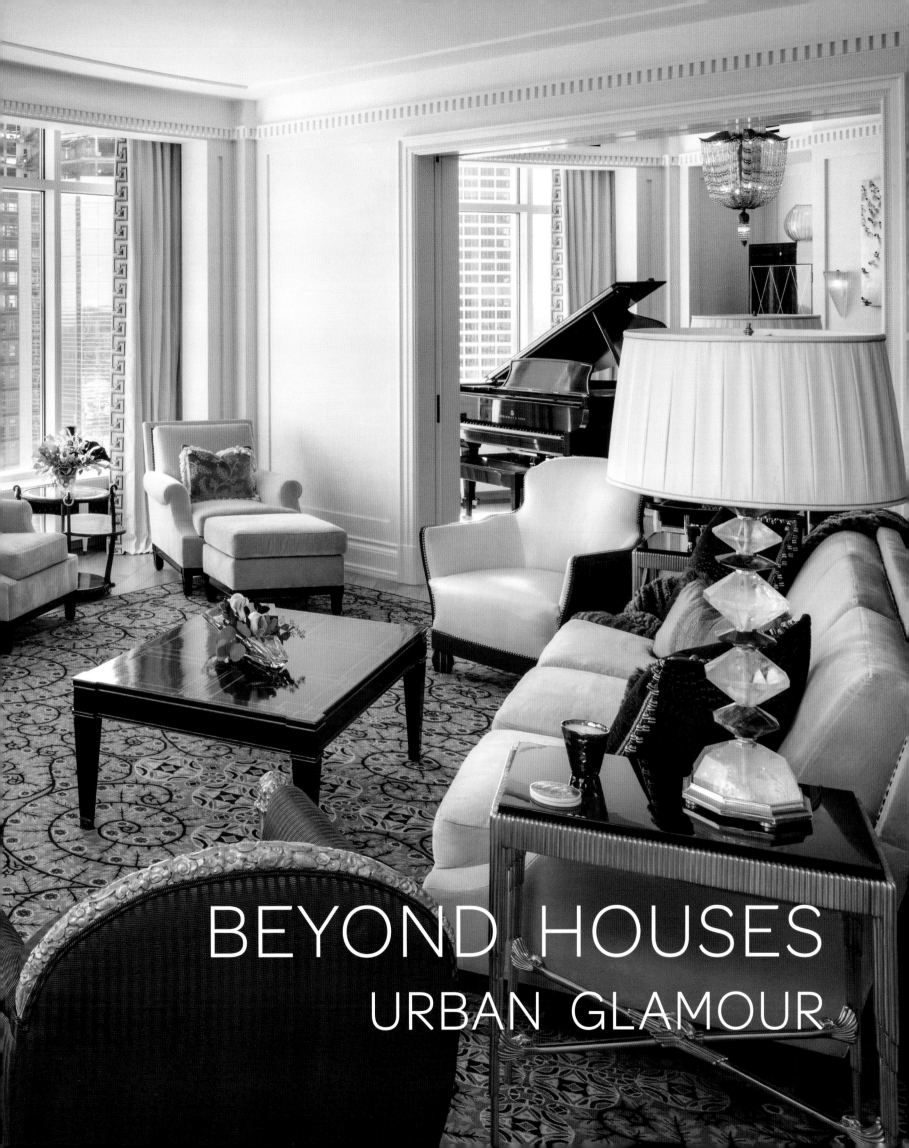

BEYOND HOUSES
URBAN GLAMOUR

CITY CHIC

Since the late 1930s, Hollywood has had a continuous love affair with the glamorous Art Deco penthouse. Fred Astaire and Ginger Rogers glided across the floors of streamlined rooms, while Joan Crawford and Rosalind Russell would get into gown-ripping catfights. No matter how traditional the story line or the characterizations, the vogue was to suggest that truly sophisticated, soigné folks lived in exquisite modern spaces that resembled ocean liners with dazzling city views.

The true beginnings of Art Deco stem from an even more finely detailed aesthetic that was presented at the International Exposition of Modern Decorative and Industrial Arts in Paris in 1925. Combining modernist styling with fine craftsmanship and rich materials, it suggested that social and technological progress should also inform luxury and glamour, creating something totally new and revolutionary.

Elements of that stylistic movement are evident in this dramatically detailed home in the clouds. Conceived not only as a luxuriously comfortable private residence but also a venue for large-scale charity events, the apartment features impressive water, sky and city views. Many of the custom architectural elements and finishes were created by the renowned Ateliers Saint-Jacques, a consortium of four workshops southwest of Paris (carpentry, ironwork, stonecutting and foundry) whose artisans have been expertly trained in the crafts necessary to reproduce heirloom-quality, mixed-media French Art Deco works. Inlay, marquetry and highly polished surfaces are everywhere, along with museum-quality modern art and period furnishings arranged in a progression of amply scaled rooms.

Cue lights and music, enter Mr. Astaire and Miss Rogers, and . . . action! Behold, a timeless residence that instantly transports all who enter back to the realm of white tie and tails, flowing, feather-trimmed gowns and, above all, effortless, graceful elegance.

This apartment boasts detailing rarely found in contemporary glass skyscrapers. From elegant inlaid floors
to artisanal paint finishes to bespoke millwork, no aspect of the space was not carefully considered.

Exclusive custom elements appear in every room, mainly in the Art Deco style and created by the legendary Atelier Saint-Jacques workshops in France.

The baths are pure Hollywood glamour, with dramatic marble tilework and a stunning mural in the alcove surrounding a luxe soaking tub.

A delightful sitting area has the feel of a sunporch, even though it is high in the sky. Delicate branches are painted on the walls to look as though they sprang organically from the veins of the Carrara marble baseboard and mantel. Chippendale-style niches hold pieces of Chinese export porcelain; this is decorative layering at its best.

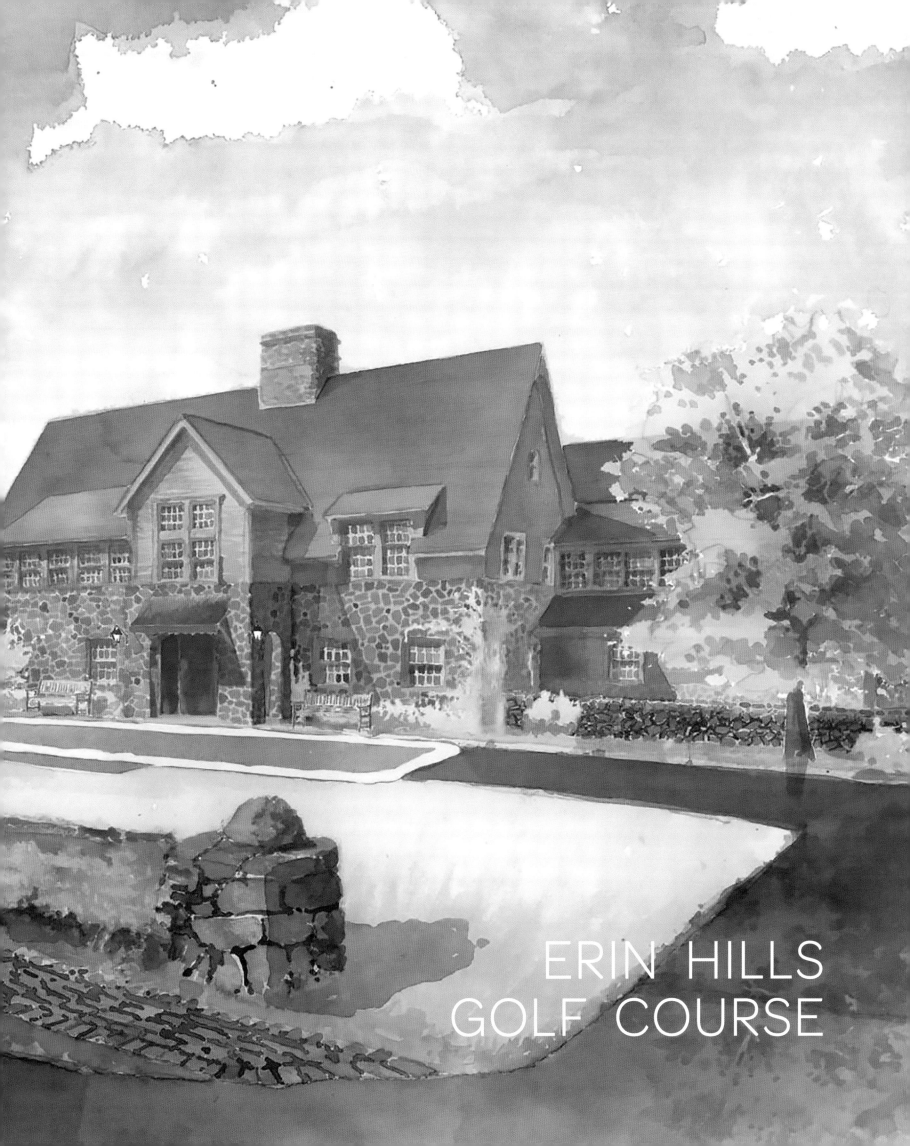

ERIN HILLS
GOLF COURSE

TRANSCENDENT TO A TEE

One of the true benefits of enlisting a firm that has an expansive residential catalog for a commercial project is that they bring to the table an understanding that the intimate scaling of a room can give it a sense of warmth that isn't always found in commercial spaces. They also comprehend the power of uniquely detailed finishes.

Such an opportunity to bring their vast experience to a commercial property came to Wade Weissmann in the form of Erin Hills, an extraordinary public golf course located thirty-five miles northwest of Milwaukee, one that famously hosted the 2017 U.S. Open. It was a thrill to create an environment that will be experienced firsthand by thousands and seen by millions.

An expansive manor house with a two-story stone fireplace is the centerpiece of the sweeping property. It functions as a traditional clubhouse, albeit marvelously open to the public, and features a variety of dining venues that all have sweeping views of the course. Eleven graciously appointed guest rooms fill out the main clubhouse. Additionally, there are five cottages with four bedrooms each, plus other support buildings, all built from natural materials in an evocative, rustic style appropriate to the landscape. Indeed, time feels suspended while at Erin Hills, whether it is veiled in the morning mist or bathed in the golden light of a Midwestern sunset; for golfers and non-golfers alike, it is an otherworldly place dedicated to the pure pleasure of the sport.

Although Erin Hills is indeed a public facility, it was detailed to feel absolutely residential and personal to all visitors. A roaring fireplace warms a cozy seating area that also features a poker table.

Spaces were designed to feature individual "nooks" that would encourage conversation. Gracious hospitality is the overwhelming theme expressed throughout the facility.

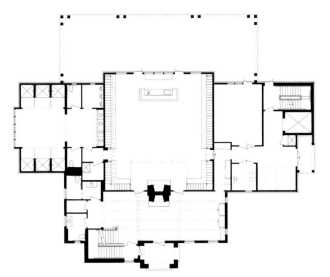

257

GERMAN
EQUESTRIAN ESTATE

WELL BRED

The passion for all things equestrian is truly one of life's rarest pursuits. It is world of extraordinary refinement and beauty combined with strength, speed and tradition. For centuries, the relationship between man and the horse has been celebrated and iconized.

This equestrian estate was inspired by the traditional farms of its location in northwestern Germany. Historical references abound, while the estate provides every possible modern convenience that a comprehensive breeding and training facility demands. The master plan features large indoor and outdoor Grand Prix rings, glorious stables and comfortable living quarters for staff, along with several outbuildings and pristine courtyards and viewing platforms.

Respectful of the surrounding gentle pastures and woodlands, the result is an expression of timelessness for a sport that knows no time.

A proper home for every horse, elegantly detailed in the tradition of the European countryside.

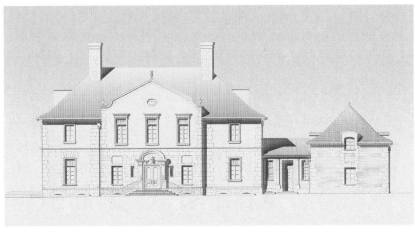

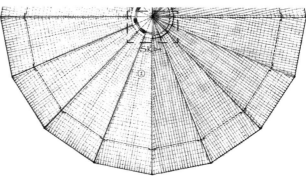

A covered rink recalls the styling of a vintage carousel, with a lyrical roofline and charming cupola. Both the drawings and the actual buildings express the feeling of total timelessness.

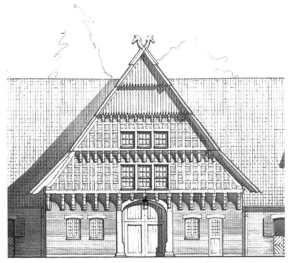

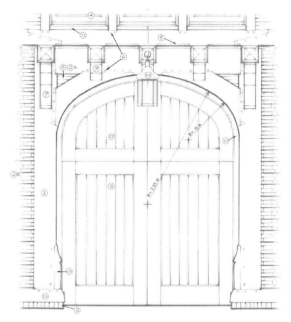

The tack room features tartan walls; an elegant juxtaposition for all the bespoke leather and brass saddlery equipment.

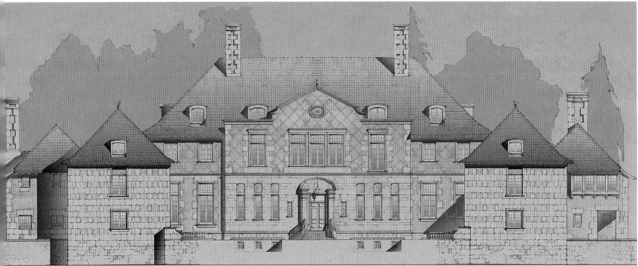

The welcoming club room features a magnificent bar and cozy seating by a large open hearth for post-riding relaxation.

22 21 20 19 18   6 5 4 3 2

Text © 2018 by Wade Weissmann Architecture

Illustrations © 2018 by Wade Weissmann Architecture

Photographic credits on page 13

Published by

Gibbs Smith

P.O. Box 667

Layton, Utah 84041

1.800.835.4993 orders

www.gibbs-smith.com

Designed by Rita Sowins / Sowins Design

Printed and bound in China

Gibbs Smith books are printed on either recycled, 100% post-consumer waste,
FSC-certified papers or on paper produced from sustainable PEFC-certified forest/controlled
wood source. Learn more at www.pefc.org.

Library of Congress Control Number: 2018930028

ISBN: 978-1-4236-4961-8